30 Days To Higher Self-Esteem *For Your Child!*

32 Letters From Karate Master Duane Brumitt to His Students & Their Parents!

By Duane K. Brumitt Jr.
© Tri-Star Martial Arts Academy 2013

www.DuaneBrumitt.com
www.TriStarKarate.com

DISCLAIMER AND TERMS OF USE AGREEMENT

The author and publisher have used their best efforts in preparing this report. The author and publisher make no representation or warranties with respect to the accuracy, applicability, fitness, or completeness of the contents of this report. The information contained in this report is strictly for educational purposes. Therefore, if you wish to apply ideas contained in this report, you are taking full responsibility for your actions.

EVERY EFFORT HAS BEEN MADE TO ACCURATELY REPRESENT THIS PRODUCT AND ITS POTENTIAL. HOWEVER, THERE IS NO GUARANTEE THAT YOU WILL IMPROVE IN ANY WAY USING THE TECHNIQUES AND IDEAS IN THESE MATERIALS. EXAMPLES IN THESE MATERIALS ARE NOT TO BE INTERPRETED AS A PROMISE OR GUARANTEE OF ANYTHING. SELF-HELP AND IMPROVEMENT POTENTIAL IS ENTIRELY DEPENDENT ON THE PERSON USING OUR PRODUCT, IDEAS AND TECHNIQUES.

YOUR LEVEL OF IMPROVEMENT IN ATTAINING THE RESULTS CLAIMED IN OUR MATERIALS DEPENDS ON THE TIME YOU DEVOTE TO THE PROGRAM, IDEAS AND TECHNIQUES MENTIONED, KNOWLEDGE AND VARIOUS SKILLS. SINCE THESE FACTORS DIFFER ACCORDING TO INDIVIDUALS, WE CANNOT GUARANTEE YOUR SUCCESS OR IMPROVEMENT LEVEL, NOR ARE WE RESPONSIBLE FOR ANY OF YOUR ACTIONS.

MANY FACTORS WILL BE IMPORTANT IN DETERMINING YOUR ACTUAL RESULTS AND NO

GUARANTEES ARE MADE THAT YOU WILL ACHIEVE RESULTS SIMILAR TO OURS OR ANYBODY ELSE'S, IN FACT NO GUARANTEES ARE MADE THAT YOU WILL ACHIEVE ANY RESULTS FROM OUR IDEAS AND TECHNIQUES IN OUR MATERIAL.

The author and publisher disclaim any warranties (express or implied), merchantability, or fitness for any particular purpose. The author and publisher shall in no event be held liable to any party for any direct, indirect, punitive, special, incidental or other consequential damages arising directly or indirectly from any use of this material, which is provided "as is", and without warranties.

As always, the advice of a competent professional should be sought.

The author and publisher do not warrant the performance, effectiveness or applicability of any sites listed or linked to in this report.

All links are for information purposes only and are not warranted for content, accuracy or any other implied or explicit purpose.

Author Duane Brumitt and his wife Debbie Brumitt on their annual St. Petersburg Fl. Vacation
(Yes, it was cold that night)

Dear Reader,

I want to tell you how proud of you I am for taking an interest in raising your child's self-esteem. Through the pages of this book I hope you find the information and inspiration to help you be the BEST parent you can be. Please let me know if I can help in any way.

ACKNOWLEDGEMENT

This book deserves a big thank you to my Mom and Dad for teaching me how to treat people and help them see the best in themselves. In fact Mom you were the best example of this. You always knew how to talk to people and listen to them as well.

A lot of my letters in this book have both my parents' wisdom in it… not to mention my former mentor Zig Ziglar. Which brings to mind one of my favorite Zig quotes, "You teach what you know but you reproduce who you are!"

Of course the wisdom of my creator God, and what I have learned about Him through His Holy Word, is a part of these letters too.

Lastly, thank you to all the parents that I have had the opportunity to "tryout" these wisdom principals on their kids before ever having mine. I had a lot of trial runs with yours before I had my own.

30 Days to Higher Self-Esteem *For Your Child!*

Table of Contents

Letter #1: To Improve Those Around You...Start With Yourself!.. 3

Letter #2: Guide Your Child Towards Success................................. 5

Letter #3: You Possess Tremendous Power................................... 8

Letter #4: Self-Esteem Strategies... 13

Letter #5: Dealing With Change 15

Letter #6: How to Raise Your Child's Self-Esteem........................ 16

Letter #7: A Dangerous Trap... 19

Letter #8: Take A Chance!... 21

Letter #9: An Urgent Message 23

Letter #10: Harmless Entertainment?.. 26

Letter #11: Be Happy! 29

Letter #12: How To Teach Your Child Anything 31

Letter #13: The "Responsibility Model"....................................... 34

Letter #14: Developing Your Child's Attention Span 37

Letter #15: Catch Your Child Doing "It" Right!............................ 40

Letter #16: Serious Games 43

Letter #17: Father Forgets 46

Letter #18: Reinforce The Positive... 49

Letter #19: "I Gotta Have It NOW!" 52

Letter #20: Positive Role Models 56

Letter #21: Powerful Self-Esteem Building Strategies 60

32 Letters From Karate Master Duane Brumitt to His Students & Their Parents!

- Letter #22: A Gentle Spirit 61
- Letter #23: Listening Skills 67
- Letter #24: Self-Esteem Killers 69
- Letter #25: Popularity Issues 71
- Letter #26: Dealing With Fear 73
- Letter #27: Five Skills For Making New Friends! 76
- Letter #28: No Substitute For Time 78
- Letter #29: Powerful Confidence 80
- Letter #30: Smell The Roses 84
- Letter #31: Pursuit Of Excellence 86
- Letter #32: A Thoughtful Review 88
- BONUS: 104 Ways To Positively Reinforce Your Child! 90
- Free Offers and Resources From Duane Brumitt 95
- Resources 102

Letter #1: To Improve Those Around You...Start With Yourself!

Dear Parent,

As you have probably noticed, one of my favorite quotes is:

"Of What Use To Make Heroic Vows of Amendment, If the Same Old Lawbreaker Is To Keep Them?" ~Ralph Waldo Emerson

This quote has a special significance for me. In the late-1990's, I began to aggressively set goals in my personal and my professional life. At the beginning of each year, I would be filled with excitement and optimism about the awesome things I was going to accomplish. And by early spring, in each of those years, it would be clear that I wasn't going to even come close to the goals that I had set. It was so discouraging!

Had I been too ambitious? Were my goals too aggressive? Were there obstacles that were too difficult to overcome? Maybe. But, about ten years ago, I had a huge breakthrough – and discovered what the problem really was.

It was me!

I was not yet the type of person who honored the commitments I made to myself! I easily lost focus. I procrastinated. I became tired and discouraged too easily.

It became clear to me that the problem wasn't that the goals were set incorrectly. It wasn't that the obstacles were too big. The problem was that I was the *"lawbreaker"* described by Emerson!

When I really got a hold of this important truth, it was easy to understand what needed to be done. I needed to work on me! Instead of setting external goals, I needed to work on becoming the type of person who honored the commitments I made to myself; to follow through; to persevere; and to maintain the energy and focus that my responsibilities require.

This was a tough truth to face. But – gaining this understanding was the key to every wonderful thing that has happened in my life over the last ten years.

Best wishes for an awesome year!

Your friend,

M. Brumitt

Master Brumitt

Letter #2: Guide Your Child Towards Success

Dear Parent,

This is an excerpt from Professor Paul Pilzer, author of "<u>Unlimited Wealth</u>" and "<u>Other People's Money</u>"... "One of the questions I am frequently asked by parents, particularly parents who have succeeded themselves but didn't have the opportunity to go to college, is what subject their son or daughter should study in college in order to achieve financial success?"

"I usually turn their question around, asking them detailed questions about what their child is really passionate about – sports, pets, movies, etc. – until they interrupt and tell me that they are asking my opinion about their child's economic welfare not their child's social life. Then I explain the answer to their original question."

"The key to achieving financial success today, or success in any field for that matter, is being able to learn new things. And the key to having the ability to learn new things is developing confidence in your ability to learn."

"Even if there were one field or another that you could study in college for financial success, it wouldn't matter because most of what you studied in school would be technologically obsolete by the time you graduated."

"Today, it doesn't matter anymore how much you already know about a particular subject – things change so quickly that the most successful people in virtually every field are the people who learn new things the fastest."

"Thus, the goal of every educational program should be to develop confidence in one's ability to learn. And the way to develop confidence about one's ability to learn is to learn something very well. And the way to learn something very well is to be passionate about learning it."

"The hope, then, for every parent concerned about their child's future economic welfare, is that the child discovers an interest in anything – music, art, history, psychology, math – that they passionately want to learn about."

"If this happens, the subject…eventually rises to the level where they will debate it with their professors."

"If, and when, this happens, their future will be set – for they will have developed confidence in their ability to learn. This confidence in their ability to learn will lead them to success in whatever they seek."

"Thus, if there is any gift a parent could give to a child, it is to nurture, whenever it occurs, the passion that a child might develop at any time to learn about any field or subject."

"For if the child masters learning just one subject, the parent who encouraged the child will have given a great gift."

"A true "gift of the magic" is a gift that keeps on giving for the rest of the child's life."

Yours for Successful Kids,

Duane Brumitt

Duane Brumitt

Letter #3: You Possess Tremendous Power

Dear Parent,

The following is one of my favorite tools in teaching the *"Duane Brumitt's Tri-Star Martial Arts Academy"* system to the teachers and assistant teachers. It easily translates to parenting skills!

Concerning a Teacher's (Parent's) Influence:

"I have come to the frightening conclusion that I am the decisive element in the classroom (home). It's my personal approach that creates the climate. It's my daily mood that makes the weather. As a teacher (parent), I possess a tremendous power to make a (my) child's life miserable or joyous. I can be a tool of torture or an instrument of inspiration. I can humiliate or humor, hurt or heal. In all situations, it is my response that decides whether a crisis will be escalated or deescalated, and a (my) child humanized or de-humanized."

The above paragraph is just a paraphrase reminder about a story that I got emailed to me just shortly after opening *"Duane Brumitt's Tri-Star Martial Arts Academy"*

It move me so much that I knew this was how I wanted to be as a teacher. If me and my instructors could teach in this fashion we would help to change thousands if not tens of thousands of our students lives during our martial arts teaching career.

If this true story doesn't make you cry you need to get your HEART checked. Tough words I know!

The Heart Test

As she stood in front of her 5th grade class on the very first day of school, she told the children an untruth. Like most teachers, she looked at her students and said that she loved them all the same. However, that was impossible, because there in the front row, slumped in his seat, was a little boy named Teddy Stoddard.

Mrs. Thompson had watched Teddy the year before and noticed that he did not play well with other children, that his clothes were messy and that he constantly needed a bath. In addition, Teddy could be unpleasant.

It got to the point where Mrs. Thompson would actually take delight in marking his papers with a broad red pen, making bold X's and then putting a big "F" at the top of his papers. At the school where Mrs. Thompson taught, she was required to review each child's past records and she put Teddy's off until last. However, when she reviewed his file, she was in for a surprise.

Teddy's first grade teacher wrote, "Teddy is a bright child with a ready laugh. He does his work neatly and has good manners...he is a joy to be around."

His second grade teacher wrote, "Teddy is an excellent student, well-liked by his classmates, but he is troubled because his mother has a terminal illness and life at home must be a struggle."

His third grade teacher wrote, "His mother's death has been hard on him. He tries to do his best, but his father doesn't show much interest and his home life will soon affect him if some steps aren't taken."

Teddy's fourth grade teacher wrote, "Teddy is withdrawn and doesn't show much interest in school. He doesn't have many friends and he sometimes sleeps in class."

By now, Mrs. Thompson realized the problem and she was ashamed of herself. She felt even worse when her students brought her Christmas presents, wrapped in beautiful ribbons and bright paper, except for Teddy's. His present was clumsily wrapped in heavy, brown paper that he got from a grocery bag. Mrs. Thompson took pains to open it in the middle of the other presents. Some of the children started to laugh when she found a rhinestone bracelet with some of the stones missing, and a bottle that was one-quarter full of perfume. But she stifled the children's laughter when she exclaimed how pretty the bracelet was, putting it on, and dabbing some of the perfume on her wrist. Teddy Stoddard stayed after school that day just long enough to say, "Mrs. Thompson, today you smelled just like my Mom used to." After the children left, she cried for at least an hour.

On that very day, she quit teaching reading, writing and arithmetic. Instead, she began to teach children. Mrs. Thompson paid particular attention to Teddy. As she worked with him, his mind seemed to come alive. The more she encouraged him, the faster he responded. By the end of the year, Teddy had become one of the smartest children in the class and, despite her lie that she would love all the children the same, Teddy became one of her "teacher's pets."

A year later, she found a note under her door, from Teddy, telling her that she was still the best teacher he ever had in his whole life.

Six years went by before she got another note from Teddy. He then wrote that he had finished high school, third in his class, and she was still the best teacher he ever had in life.

Four years after that, she got another letter, saying that whilst things had been tough at times, he'd stayed in school, had stuck with it, and would soon graduate from college with the highest of honors. He assured Mrs. Thompson that she was still the best and favorite teacher he had ever had in his whole life.

Then four more years passed and yet another letter came. This time he explained that after he got his bachelor's degree, he decided to go a little further. The letter explained that she was still the best and favorite teacher he ever had. But now his name was a little longer...The letter was signed, Theodore F. Stoddard, MD.

The story does not end there. You see, there was yet another letter that spring. Teddy said he had met this girl and was going to be married. He explained that his father had died a couple of years ago and he was wondering if Mrs. Thompson might agree to sit at the wedding in the place that was usually reserved for the mother of the groom.

Of course, Mrs. Thompson did. And guess what? She wore the bracelet, the one with several rhinestones missing. Moreover, she made sure she was wearing the perfume that Teddy remembered his mother wearing on their last Christmas together.

They hugged each other, and Dr. Stoddard whispered in Mrs. Thompson's ear, "Thank you Mrs. Thompson for believing in me. Thank you so much for making me feel important and showing me that I could make a difference."

Mrs. Thompson, with tears in her eyes, whispered back. She said, "Teddy, you have it all wrong. You were the one who taught me that I could make a difference. I didn't know how to teach until I met you!."

(For those of you who don't know, Teddy Stoddard is the Dr. at Iowa Methodist in Des Moines that has the Stoddard Cancer Wing.)

Yours for Successful Kids,

Duane Brumitt

Letter #4: Self-Esteem Strategies

Dear Parent,

Please consider carefully the following strategies:

3 Tips for Developing Self-Discipline in Your Children

1. Always, always, do what you say you are going to do. Remember that your children learn from EVERY encounter with you…even if it's not what you want them to learn! If you tell a child that a certain behavior will cause them to be punished, you MUST follow through with the punishment. Each time you don't follow through, you teach your child, "Mom and Dad don't mean what they say."

   If a child, for example, is being disruptive, and you say, "Michael, please stop that," and then allow Michael to continue, you have effectively taught Michael to disobey! Additionally, children need the security that comes from knowing Mom and Dad are truly in charge. Any inconsistency in your approach robs them of that security!

2. Show your children the effects of self-discipline, and the effects of LACK of self-discipline. Be on the lookout for people who are becoming successful as a result of their self-discipline. Family members, athletes, famous people, even fictional characters can be great examples. In the same way, show your children the results of the lack of self-discipline. Discuss people who are in

trouble, or people who don't get the results they want, and show your children how the breakdown in their self-discipline led them to trouble!

3. Paint an exciting future for your children. Inspire them to dream big dreams, to think boldly about their future. Show them the opportunities that become available to people who have great discipline!

   Follow these tips, and your child will develop the important quality of Self-Discipline!

   Yours for Successful Kids,

   Duane Brumitt

   Duane Brumitt

Letter #5: Dealing With Change

Dear Parent,

Change can be upsetting. We get used to doing things certain ways…and then something changes! We feel inconvenienced, or threatened, or somehow certain that things won't be as good as they once were.

And, yet, somehow things always seem to stabilize. The comfort level we feel with the "old" way is relative. Because, before the "old" way – it used to be a different way. And the old way was once the new, uncomfortable way.

Whether we like it or not, changes continue to come. About the only thing that doesn't change is that things DO Change!

We apologize for any inconvenience recent changes may have caused you. Every one of them was done sincerely, and with the best interests of the whole school at heart.

And, if you can (and not just at *"Duane Brumitt's Tri-Star Martial Arts Academy"*), relax and enjoy the journey. Change usually brings unexpected, pleasant surprises.

Your Friend,

M. Brumitt

Master Brumitt

Letter #6: How to Raise Your Child's Self-Esteem

Dear Parents,

Beware! There is a thief near you! And that thief is not after your money or your IPad. This thief is after something far more valuable.

The thief is after the Self-Esteem of your most precious gift…your child.

My friends, we live in a largely negative world and, unless you are vigilant, that negativity will drain the Self-Esteem from your son or daughter.

Protecting the Self-Esteem of your child is an ongoing, never-ending task. The responsibility falls to you. If you don't undertake this urgent responsibility, who will?

The *"Duane Brumitt's Tri-Star Martial Arts Academy"* teachers use a 10 step approach to developing and protecting Self-Esteem.

You can use these strategies, too!

> 1. Always remind your child of their past victories and accomplishments. Let their self-image be built upon a recollection of past successes. Let

the memory of failures and disappointments fade away.

2. Help your child strive for improvement…not perfection. Help them to create reasonable expectations for performance.

3. Develop a family heritage. Teach your child to be proud of your family. Tell them about the achievements and sacrifices of their parents, grandparents, and other relatives.

4. Do provide feedback. Don't be overly critical. If you do have to give negative feedback, especially to an older child, always criticize privately and always praise publicly!

5. Teach them the value of telling the truth. Lying steals Self-Esteem!

6. Appearances count! Guide your child into taking pride in their appearance.

7. Try to guide them toward friends who have high Self-Esteem. Help them to avoid negative people.

8. Paint the big picture with your child. Help her to dream big dreams about her future!

9. Be healthy, exercise regularly and eat a balanced diet.

10. Become an expert! Pick a couple of activities that are important to your child and help him to MASTER them! Don't allow them to float from activity to activity.

If you have questions about Self-Esteem issues, give me a call. I will be happy to help! **815-932-5425**

Your Friend,

Duane Brumitt

Letter #7: A Dangerous Trap...

Dear Parent,

This appeared in an Ann Landers column on 7/21/86

Dear Ann Landers,

"I first met her in high school. She was older than I, and exciting. She'd been around. My Parents warned me to have nothing to do with her. They claimed no good could come from our relationship."

"But I kept meeting her on the sly. She was so sophisticated and worldly. It made me feel grown up just being with her. It was fun to take her to a party in those days. She was almost always the center of attention."

"We began seeing more of each other after I started college. When I got a place of my own, she was a frequent guest. It wasn't long before she moved in with me. It was heartbreaking for my parents, but I kept reminding myself I wasn't a kid anymore. Besides, it was legal."

"We lived together right through college and into my early days in business. I seldom went anywhere without her, but I wasn't blind. I knew she was unfaithful to me. What's worse, I didn't care. As long as she was there for me when I needed her (and she always was) it didn't matter."

"The longer we lived together, the more attached I became to her. But it wasn't mutual. She began to delight in making me look foolish in front of my friends. But still I couldn't give her up. It became a love-hate relationship. I figured out that her glamour was nothing more than a cheap-mask to hide her spite and cynicism. I could no longer see her beauty after I came to know her true character."

"But old habits are hard to break. We had invested many years in each other. Even though my relationship with her made me lose a little respect for myself, she had become the center of my life. We didn't go anywhere. We didn't do anything. We didn't have friends over. It was just the two of us. I became deeply depressed and knew that she was largely responsible for my misery. I finally told her I was leaving for good. It took a lot of guts but I left."

"I still see her around. I still miss her now and then. I'm not boasting when I say she'd take me back in a minute. But by the grace of God, I will never take up with her again."

"If you see her, give her my regards. I don't hate her. I just loved her too much".

"Chances are you know her family. The name is Alcohol."

Yours for Successful Kids,

Duane Brumitt

Letter #8: Take A Chance!

Dear Student,

This is one of my favorite articles. It's by Tom Peters, the author of "In Search of Excellence," and "Passion for Excellence."

"Risk Taking: Let's say you were playing poker and you thought you had a decent hand. In fact, you were willing to bet on it! Out of your five poker chips, you bet two. And guess what? Somebody has a better hand, and you lose your two chips! Now, you better be more careful next time, right?"

"Did you know that many people are terrified of taking risks. Terrified to the point that they avoid trying new things? They avoid doing the very things that lead to real growth!"

"Well, if all risk taking were like that poker game, you would do well to be cautious, and avoid risk."

"But let's consider a different poker game. Again you are dealt a pretty good hand. You like your chances, so, once again, you bet two chips. The cards are laid down, and again, you lose!"

"But this time, something different happens. As the winner scoops up the pot, the dealer hands you two chips, to replace the ones you have lost! And, much to your astonishment, each time you lose, your supply of chips is replenished!"

"You begin playing more aggressively. Your confidence soars when you discover that each chance leaves you no worse off than when you started."

And you know what happens?

"Sometimes you're going to win. And I suggest that, because of your newly found confidence, and your aggressive style of play, you win more often than ever before!"

"Well, are there any of us who wouldn't like to be in that second poker game where you always had a chance to hit the jackpot and no chance of loss if you failed?"

"There is one thing, however, that is guaranteed. It is a sure thing that if you don't take any risks, if you don't try anything new in your life, you will always get the same results you are getting right now!"

"The only way to truly lose is by doing nothing…so…go for it! You will do well, students, to give some thought to how this applies in your life!"

Yours for Success,

M. Brumitt

Master Brumitt

Letter #9: An Urgent Message

Dear Parent,

It's been a while since we have run a *"How to Raise a Juvenile Delinquent"* class.

Its tone is somewhat harsh…but the directness of the message speaks to the urgency of mastering these simple lessons…

"How to Raise a Juvenile Delinquent"

1. Begin from infancy to give the child everything they want. In this way, they will grow up to believe that the world owes them a living.

2. When the child picks up bad words, laugh at them. It will encourage them to pick up other phrases that will blow the top off your head later.

3. Never give them any spiritual training. Wait until they are 21 and let them decide for themself.

4. Avoid the use of the word "wrong." It may develop a guilt complex. This will condition them to believe later, when they are arrested for stealing a car, that society is against them and that they are being persecuted.

30 Days to Higher Self-Esteem *For Your Child!*

5. Pick up everything they leave lying around – books, shoes, and clothes. Do everything for them so they will be experienced in throwing the responsibility onto others.

6. Let them read any printed material that they can get their hands on. Be careful that their silverware and drinking glasses are sterilized, but let their mind feed on garbage.

7. Quarrel frequently in the presence of the children. Then they won't be shocked when the home is broken up.

8. Give the child all the spending money they want. Never let them earn their own. Why should they have things as tough as you had them?

9. Satisfy their every craving for food, drink, and comfort. See that every desire is gratified. Denial may lead to harmful frustration.

10. Take their side against the neighbors, teachers, and policemen. They are all prejudiced against your child.

11. When they get in real trouble, apologize for yourself by saying, "I never could do anything with him/her."

12. Prepare for a life of grief. You'll have it.

Like I said friends – tough words…but I think you'll agree – they hit the bulls eye!

>Your friend,
>
>Duane Brumitt

Letter #10: Harmless Entertainment?

Dear Fellow Parents,

A kid's movie comes out, and everybody is talking about it. Your children tell you that practically everybody in their class has seen it. So, on a Saturday afternoon, you pack the kids up, grab a rather large wad of cash – and off you go to the local movie theater. You can tell the kids are excited by the happy look on their faces and you are too. You remember what a special event it was to attend a movie when you were a kid, and you look forward to sharing that experience with your kids!

The lights finally dim, and the movie starts. And, before 10 minutes have gone by, you cringe as the first in a long series of profane words, thinly veiled sexual references, and bathroom humor unfolds.

Whether you are in a theater, or at home watching rental movies…we've all had this happen, haven't we? Things that, when I was growing up, would have been considered shocking in grownup films, are now considered to be acceptable in kid's films!

When my older two were young, and we were exposed to this – it made me mad! What gave these movie makers the right to lure us into the theater with the promise of a "kid-type" movie…and then embarrass my family with objectionable content? What gave them the right to make it look like I approved of this type of thing…just by being in attendance!

Now – I'm not a prude, and I'm sure you are not, either. If grownups want to watch movies that have this type of content…so be it.

But I have a question, and I have a concern.

My question is…WHY? Why do film makers consider it necessary to include this type of content in children's movies? If the goal is to train them early, and desensitize them…so that, as adults, they will be accepting of content that is even more crude, more crass…those film makers are right on track.

My concern, of course, is what this does to the Self-Esteem of our children? The "big screen" is powerful. Just as a well written, uplifting movie can have a profoundly positive, enlightening impact on the viewer…so can a movie that shows the human spirit at its worst, lower the moral values and the Self-Esteem of the viewer.

You see, whatever your child sees on the screen becomes accepted as normal, right, and acceptable. And, as Mom and Dad sit in silence, cringing, we implicitly put our stamp of approval on what is being watched.

Movie content has gotten progressively worse over the last 30 years…very gradually. We have gotten used to profanity, sexual references, and bad behavior in the movies a little bit at a time. They didn't dump all of this type of stuff on us all at once. Nobody would have tolerated that. If you throw a frog into a pot of boiling water, he immediately jumps out. But put him into a nice, lukewarm pot of water, and he becomes comfortable. He relaxes, as you steadily, gradually, turn up the heat. And – before he knows it – he's frog soup!

So…what to do? You can choose, of course, to go head to head with the studios; boycott the advertisers; write angry letters. These things are OK, and it's important that they are done.

But you don't have to solve the industry problem to resolve this issue within your family. As a parent, you are entitled to stand firm against this type of content. Let your kids know, "Our family does NOT tolerate these things in the movies any more than we tolerate them in real life!"

Does this mean that you have to insist that everything that your family sees is "squeaky clean?" Well – you be the judge. But my question is…why not? Why not adopt a "zero tolerance" policy for ANYTHING that reduces the Self-Esteem of your Child?

There are plenty of movie options with no objectionable content whatsoever.

Yours for Successful Kids,

Duane Brumitt

Letter #11: Be Happy!

Dear Parent,

Be happy! Focus each day on joy. Don't wait for everything to be perfect. There will always be things that seem less than perfect. Don't let worry and stress steal your joy!

Have you ever worried about something and said to yourself, "I'll be so happy when I get past this hurdle; then I can relax and be happy!"

Then, when you DO get past that particular hurdle, instead of relaxing and being happy…your brain seeks out some new thing to worry about!

If you have ever had this experience, you can see that it is a pattern of your brain – to seek out the next thing to worry about.

But it doesn't have to work this way. Once you become aware of the "seeking nature" of your brain, you can, with some simple mental discipline, train your brain to focus on the next thing that will make you happy!

And – truthfully now – how many of those things that you were worried about actually happened? Probably very few! And – of the small number that did actually happen…how much did your worrying help?

Worry and stress - not only do they steal your joy in the present. If left unchecked, they eventually kill you.

Master this area of your life…before it "masters" you!

One verse of scripture that always helps me out is Philippians 4:6-7

"6 Do not be anxious about anything, but in every situation, by prayer and petition, with thanksgiving, present your requests to God. 7 And the peace of God, which transcends all understanding, will guard your hearts and your minds in Christ Jesus."

        Your friend,

        M. Brumitt

        Master Brumitt

Letter #12: How To Teach Your Child Anything

Dear Parent,

We have a *"method"* that most people say is crazy.

You will notice that your child's Karate teachers understand that in order to build self-esteem, they cannot be too concerned about performance…in the beginning!

I know our methods seem "crazy," because they sometimes elicit these types of comments:

"My child doesn't seem to be trying!" "She never wants to practice!" "I look at the other students techniques, and my child's seem so sloppy by comparison!"

Occasionally, I hear comments like these from the parents of beginning students. They compare their child's performance to that of other (often, more experienced) students, and feel that their child is not doing well.

There is a tendency, of course, to look at our own children through a microscope…analyzing each technique, each individual effort…and, often, watching carefully in case any negative behavior appears.

It's hard for a young child, with a normal, age appropriate, wandering attention span, to withstand such scrutiny.

I'd like to raise another point, however. I have virtually never had a parent bring a child to our school, and say, "I want my child to be an expert Martial Art practitioner or the next Bruce Lee."

It is more typical that a parent comes to our school and says, "I've heard you can improve my child's self-esteem." Or, "We've heard that you do wonders with children's focus."

In other words, parents tend to bring children to our school because they want them to **benefit**… not because they want them to be great performers.

It becomes easy, though, to focus on performance…because that is what you are looking at when you watch your child in class…even though that's not what you brought your child to *"Duane Brumitt's Tri-Star Martial Arts Academy"* for.

So…here's my point: Your child's ability to perform in class has absolutely NOTHING to do with whether or not he or she is benefitting!

Our "crazy" methods WILL build your child's self-esteem. So – my suggestion is that you watch carefully for signs that your child is BENEFITTING from the lessons.

Is Marcus gradually becoming more respectful around the house? Easier to get along with? Is Heather sometimes listening a little more closely to what you say?

Is Amber becoming a little more courageous about trying new things?

When we discovered this "crazy method," we were, of course, pleased.

Imagine how pleased we were when we discovered that there was a bonus benefit to this system: that kids with improving self-esteem become excellent Karate practitioners.

Just take a look at our Black Belts. You will see what I mean.

Yours for successful kids,

M. Brumitt

Master Brumitt

Letter #13: The "Responsibility Model"

Dear Parent,

Responsibility! How many times have you said to yourself, "I wish my child would be more RESPONSIBLE!???"

As parents we want our children to grow up to be responsible for themselves. This includes taking responsibility for their actions, commitments, outcomes, and decisions.

When your child was born, you assumed full responsibility for them. Over the next 20 years, your job, your responsibility, is to gradually turn that responsibility over to them!

Teaching your child to be responsible takes time and attention from you. Every bit of responsibility you give your child must come with a tremendous amount of instruction and supervision. To raise a responsible child, you must be prepared to teach, remind, and inspect…over and over…a zillion times. And you must be prepared to do this without becoming frustrated, impatient, or resentful.

The following is a "model" that you can follow to teach your child how to handle responsibility.

The "Responsibility Model"

1. Assign a task. Teach what is expected, and how to meet those expectations.
2. Provide an opportunity to work on the task.
3. Before completion, inspect and provide constructive feedback.
4. If your child's efforts were successful, great! Just continue with Step #3. If your child's results weren't quite successful, go back to Step #1.

Notice that, if your child's efforts weren't successful, you don't take away the responsibility. It just means they need a little more teaching and more frequent feedback. If this happens, you must be patient and supportive! If you appear disappointed or impatient, your child will become discouraged and resentful.

Sound like a lot of work? It is! Is it really necessary? Yup – Absolutely!

Many times, parents are surprised by the level of commitment that it takes to teach a child how to be responsible. They become frustrated and stop trying.

If you give up, or if you skip steps in the "Responsibility Model," chances are that your child won't be able to effectively handle responsibility.

It's a huge mistake to assume that our children will grow up to be responsible adults without a tremendous amount of coaching.

So parents, be diligent. Use the model. Don't become frustrated or give up. Stick with it and your child will learn to handle all types of responsibility effectively!

If you have questions about helping your child handle RESPONSIBILITY, give me a call at **815-932-5425**. I'd be glad to help!

Your friend,

M. Brumitt

Master Brumitt

Letter #14: Developing Your Child's Attention Span

Dear Parent,

Short attention spans don't stand a chance in our classroom!

I recently read that children's attention spans don't exceed 10 minutes – and I'm sure many parents will agree! However, while some might see this as a limitation, we see it as useful information in structuring our classroom.

Psychologists have recommended that teachers break up their classes into smaller segments, because the study had revealed that children tend to "retain" more information at the beginning and at the end of a learning session.

We took that to heart…By now, you have probably noticed that in our classes, the children never work on any one skill for more than a few minutes. If you watch, you'll see that the kids don't even stay with the same teacher for more than about 10 minutes. At first glance it may appear to be chaos with the kids moving back and forth in the classroom!

However, there is a purpose to this "craziness." At the beginning of each class, the students line up, bow in, and do a quick warm-up. As the children are stretching after their warm-up, the head instructor begins to divide the class by age or rank.

Each of the other instructors has a different part of the lesson plan – it might be forms, basics, self-defense, rolls & falls, or any number of drills – and each is given a small group of children to work with.

After a few minutes, you'll hear the head instructor yell "One minute, teachers!" This is the cue for each instructor to finish their drill and prepare to send their group to the next teacher.

The kids are sent off to another part of the room, with a new teacher and a new drill, just as their attention span had reached its limit with the old drill. A short attention span isn't given a fair chance when faced with the combination of this "switch" and the "SSL" rule.

"SSL," by the way, stands for "Sweating, Smiling and Learning." In other words, our students are learning an important skill at the same time that they're getting a good workout…and having a good time. And balance is the key to accomplishing our goal of improving our students' lives.

We get much better results when we have a good balance between teaching kids life skills, giving them a good workout, and making sure they have a great time when they come to class. If we only focused on one aspect of the class - "sweating," for example - the kids wouldn't want to come. If we didn't teach the kids valuable life skills, the parents wouldn't be interested in bringing their children.

After all…what keeps us interested in working with children is seeing the benefits of their training – improved self-esteem, confidence, respect, courage, integrity, and perseverance. And these are the things that keep parents interested.

Yours for successful kids,

M. Brumitt

Master Brumitt

Letter #15: Catch Your Child Doing "It" Right!

Dear Parent,

The other day I saw a father talking to his daughter after she finished her karate class. It was easy to see that he loved his daughter and wanted her to do well, but his desire to see her do well was the very thing that made her feel like a failure – like she couldn't do anything right. The girl looked like she wanted to run off and cry.

Children, more than anything else, want to be loved and appreciated – especially by busy parents. The amount of approval a child gets from their parents is often the measuring stick by which the child gauges how much they are loved. That's why children often check to see if Mom and Dad are watching.

As grown-ups, we know how important it is for our children to pay attention while they're in class…to not miss any piece of information that could be critical to their success. As loving parents, we want our children to do well.

And that's where the mistake is often made – kids looking up to see if mom and dad are watching, are sometimes met with a scowl and a quick gesture to turn around and pay attention to the instructor, when all they were looking for was a smile and a thumbs up.

Of course, parents would be horrified to learn that they were unintentionally hurting their child – out of concern and love! None of our "Karate Parents" want to see their children's self-esteem dashed.

You see, people (and children especially!) learn much more efficiently and stay more focused when they are praised for doing something right, rather than criticized for doing something wrong. Children will have the confidence to move out of their comfort zone when they know that they are encouraged and free from criticism.

Parents who want to support their children in class will have the most success when giving their child a quick thumbs up and encouraging their child – loving them with their smile!

Making corrections is the instructor's second most important job – please leave it up to us!

You see, developing life skills in children is our number one priority and when working with kids, it's important to "put first things first" – striving for long term benefits like Black Belt Excellence, a strong self-image, respect, courage, modesty, perseverance, and integrity.

Making corrections in the physical side of the Martial Arts (stances, techniques, etc.) is our second most important job. Especially in the beginning!

We were very excited to learn that this "first things first" system also brings about a very positive side effect.

Just think how excited we were when we realized that when we put positive character development first, excellent physical Martial Arts skills followed! When our teachers "put first things first," the physical skills of the Martial Arts eventually develop to exciting levels!

Just take a look at our Black Belts. You will see what I mean.

Yours for Successful Kids,

M. Brumitt

Master Brumitt

P.S. If you have a concern about your child's progress, mistakes, attention span, or behavior while in class (or out of class, for that matter); I encourage you to privately express your concerns with myself or one of our instructors. It's not good for your child's self-esteem to openly criticize them or an instructor – especially in front of your child!

Letter #16: Serious Games

Dear Parent,

Some parents are amused by it, and others just think it's silly. Still, others are just curious why. We often get asked: "Why do your teachers take the games you play in the classroom so seriously?"

Chances are, you've seen your child play one of our favorite games, in which her goal is to remain standing perfectly still as one of the teachers creates all of the distractions they can think of. You've probably felt yourself pulling for your child, hoping she could remain still.

Deep inside, everyone has a place that is immovable, determined, and focused. Some people call it the "do what it takes" or the "go the distance" attitude. It's often referred to as discipline or commitment – but we consider it the root of both. And we call it, "Having a Whatever it Takes Attitude!"

Fortunately, most children have not had the kinds of experiences that would force them to dig that deep…Yet!

Some kids find it when dealing with a tough coach in high school football or when dealing with an injury (either physical or emotional). Some unfortunate kids never find that place.

But what if there was a way that would help kids find that place that was safe and fun? What if there was a way of finding it that children looked forward to, and were motivated to chart their progress? A way that was completely painless yet was so effective it must be "magical?"

We call this "magical" way the "Attention Stance Game" or "Freeze Like A Popsicle But Just Don't Melt Game". It's not a hard game for kids to learn –as they try their hardest to stand at attention, perfectly still, the teachers use any means of distraction (except tickling or touching), some of which are quite silly, to try to get the kids to move. If a child loses concentration, they are asked to sit off to the side, or do a few exercises. The teacher's goal is to make all of the kids laugh – and the child's goal is to be the last one standing.

If you watch, you'll notice that the beginning students are usually the first ones to break concentration. But as they continue through the belt ranks, students learn how to reach that place of deep inner strength, and are able to remain at attention longer. By the time a student reaches red belt or so, the teachers almost never win!

That is the best part of the "Attention Stance Game" – when the kids win, and the teachers "lose" – the kids and the teachers *both* win. Obviously, the kids have won the game. But the teachers have won the battle of leading students to that deep, inner place where they find commitment and discipline.

And the process is FUN, for both the kids and the teachers!

We all love "Win-Win" situations – especially when it means that our students are learning such valuable lessons.

30 Days to Higher Self-Esteem *For Your Child!*

The lessons learned in the "Attention Stance Game" are right at the core of positive character development.

We love using games in the classroom because they are so powerful when it comes to teaching character development. That's why you'll notice that a part of our classes are dedicated to playing games.

All of our games, in fact, have an underlying lesson. As you watch your child's karate class, are you able to figure out what the lesson is behind the game?

Yours for Successful Kids,

M. Brumitt
Master Brumitt

Letter #17: Father Forgets

Dear Parent,

"Father Forgets" is one of my favorite "reminder" stories. I thought you might enjoy it, too.

Father Forgets

Listen, Son: I am saying this as you lie asleep, one little paw crumpled under your cheek and the blond curls stickily wet on your damp forehead. I have stolen into your room alone. Just a few minutes ago, as I sat reading my paper in the library, a stifling wave of remorse had swept over me. Guiltily, I came to your bedside.

These are the things I was thinking, Son: I had been cross with you. I scolded you as you were dressing for school because you gave your face merely a dab with a towel. I took you to task for not cleaning your shoes. I called out angrily when you threw some of your things on the floor.

At breakfast I found fault, too. You spilled things. You gulped down your food. You put your elbows on the table. You spread butter too thick on your bread. And as you started off to play and I made for my train, you turned and waved a hand and called, "Good-bye, Daddy!" and I frowned, and said in reply, "Hold your shoulders back!"

Then it began all over again in the late afternoon. As I came up the road I spied you, down on your knees, playing marbles. There were holes in your stockings. I humiliated you before your friends by marching you ahead of me to the house. Stockings were expensive – and if you had to buy them you would be more careful! Imagine that, Son, from a father!

Do you remember, later, when I was reading in the library, how you came in, timidly, with a sort of hurt look in your eyes? When I glanced up over my paper, impatient at the interruption, you hesitated at the door. "What is it you want?" I snapped.

You said nothing, but ran across in one tempestuous plunge and threw your arms around my neck and kissed me, and your small arms tightened with an affection that God had set blooming in your heart and which even neglect could not wither. And then you were gone, pattering up the stairs.

Well, Son, it was shortly afterwards that my paper slipped from my hands and a terrible sickening fear came over me. What has habit been doing to me? The habit of finding fault, of reprimanding – this was my reward to you for being a boy. It was not that I did not love you; it was that I expected too much of youth. I was measuring you by the yardstick of my own years.

And there was so much that was good and fine and true in your character. The little heart of you was as big as dawn itself over the wide hills. This was shown by your spontaneous impulse to come in and kiss me good-night. Nothing else matters tonight, Son. I have come to your bedside in the darkness, and I have knelt there ashamed!

It is a feeble atonement; I know you would not understand these things if I told them to you during your waking hours. But tomorrow I will be a real daddy! I will chum with you, and suffer when you suffer, and laugh when you laugh. I will bite my tongue when impatient words come. I will keep saying as if it were a ritual: "He is nothing but a boy – a little boy!"

I am afraid I have visualized you as a man. Yet as I see you now, Son crumpled and weary in your cot, I see that you are still a baby. Yesterday you were in your mother's arms, your head on her shoulder. I have asked too much, too much.

By W. Livingston Larned

Yours for Successful Kids,

Duane Brumitt

Letter #18: Reinforce The Positive

Dear Parents,

As you already know, discipline is an important part of our classes here at *"Duane Brumitt's Tri-Star Martial Arts Academy."* We believe that it is critically important for our students to learn discipline in the classroom – so that they will have discipline in all areas of their lives. As we teach this important life skill, our students develop two types of discipline: External and Internal.

External discipline is the kind that is imposed on one person by another. Once I was at a ball game when I saw external discipline at its extreme – a mother was yelling at her son for spilling his soda…her veins were popping out of her neck, and the mean expression on her face was only intensified when she turned bright red.

This mom brought back memories of a teacher I once had, who was very strict, and always lost her temper. She was quick to yell and to take away fun things like recess, giving us instead lengthy assignments.

External discipline has one advantage – it gets immediate results. The recipients will quickly fall into line out of fear of punishment. However, the down side is that external discipline is often short term. Some psychologists even feel that external discipline will leave long-term scars!

Here at *"Duane Brumitt's Tri-Star Martial Arts Academy,"* we believe that all people, especially kids…deep down inside…want to do the right thing. It's just that children sometimes get distracted, or become caught up in the moment, and forget to do what is right.

On the other hand, Self-Disciplined people, or people who have internal discipline, always do the right thing – without someone else telling them what to do. A person with internal discipline can work by themselves without being supervised. This is a sign of positive character development.

So, how is self-discipline developed? We have figured out a way that, over time, works wonders!

The answer is so obvious…that it's hard to see!

Picture a small group of kids sitting and listening to the karate teacher. One little boy begins to bother the kid next to him, poking him in the arm.

An external disciplinarian (like my old teacher) would quickly point at the child and say, in a sharp tone, "Stop that!"

There are two problems with this response. First, it focuses the attention of the entire group on a behavior that we don't want. But even worse – it dashes the self-esteem of the misbehaving child – and in many cases, poor self-esteem is the cause of the misbehavior! Here, the teacher did get immediate results – but did nothing to impact the long-term behavior of the student.

Let's look at another scenario. This time, instead of drawing attention to the misbehaving student, the teacher looks for a child who demonstrates good self-disciplined behavior and publicly praises the child, saying things like

30 Days to Higher Self-Esteem *For Your Child!*

"You are a super listener!" The other students quickly "straighten up," and the teacher compliments them as well, being sure to include the student who was misbehaving.

By drawing attention to the attentive child – and making an example of *good* behavior, the teacher improves that student's self-esteem – instead of taking the misbehaving student's self-esteem down a notch.

It works just as quickly, and is more effective than the external methods!

The only challenge is that it requires the teacher to be more patient, creative, and attentive.

And best of all, when done consistently, the misbehaving children are taught what to do (instead of what not to do.) Their self-esteem is improved, rather than dashed…and, over time, they become self-disciplined – and that lasts a lifetime!

A self-disciplined person not only knows what to do…but does it.

Yours for Successful Kids,

M. Brumitt

Master Brumitt

P.S. Please don't get me wrong, there is a time and a place for a reprimand – it is after positive reinforcement has failed – and should be done privately. We are big believers in "Public Praise and Private Reprimand."

Letter #19: "I Gotta Have It NOW!"

Dear Parents,

Every parent, at one time or another, has asked their children to stop playing and come do something else, whether it's cleaning up, eating dinner, or going to karate class. And every parent has experienced the resistance a child can raise when asked to change activities.

You see, there is one source which drives children's life management skills – Instant Gratification. Children are so caught up in what they are doing – right now – that they are unable to realize that anything else matters.

If it was up to them, kids wouldn't do anything except those things that are fun and exciting to them.

Now, as adults, we all know that there are other things which exist and matter. We have learned that instant gratification is no way to determine the path of our lives (except for some adults who seem to be stuck in "terminal childhood!").

I personally know two adults who illustrate this point. The first was fortunate to have parents who played an active role in his character development. They helped to mold his future and were involved with his responsibilities, such as homework, youth groups, and other activities. They taught him to handle these responsibilities effectively.

Of course, like any other child, he did not always want to do his homework. He didn't always feel like leaving his friends to go to karate either. But he did go on to earn his

Black Belt from *"Duane Brumitt's Tri-Star Martial Arts Academy."* By the time he had graduated high school, he had earned his 2nd Degree Black Belt, and now he is in the final stages of college!

The second person only wanted to do things that were fun. Whenever his parents asked him to do something that he considered boring, he would put up such a fuss that eventually his parents would give in. They were tired of arguing with him.

He never wanted to do anything constructive – he'd rather watch TV or play with his friends. By the time he reached junior high, he and his friends had too much time on their hands and often wound up in trouble. It was all quite fun for him – but obviously, it wasn't productive at all. In high school, he learned how to skip classes without getting caught – they were too boring for him.

Both of these young men are the same age. The first is excited about the opportunities that lie ahead, and can't wait to get into the "real world" and help people. The second, on the other hand, is in the "real world" and can't keep track of how many jobs he's had. He has no real education, is always short on money, has no plans for the future, and is not happy.

Thinking about these two young men reminds me of what Mark Twain once said: "If you think education is expensive…try ignorance." Someday, these young men will probably have children and hopefully they'll take the time to mold their children's future.

As concerned parents, we must be able to see things that other parents can't. We must be able to look at the big picture and put our children's desires into perspective. Not only do we need to teach our kids to plan for the future, we also have to do everything we can to keep them focused, active and productive.

Even parents who do "everything right" won't necessarily have the "perfect child." But the "perfect child" hardly EVER comes from a family who doesn't take the time to teach, guide, and nurture their child even forcing them to do the things which are in their best long-term interest.

Two times a year we have black belt testing and at the end of each test I ask what I think is a very interesting question…and below is the response I get every time.

"How many of you felt like quitting at some point on your journey to black belt…but your parents wouldn't let you?" One child slowly raised his hand…then another, and another, and before long, each child had a hand up.

Then I ask another question… "How many of you are glad you stuck it out?" Each child always shoots their hands up high!

No doubt, there will be a time when your child will put up a fuss about going to karate. They won't want to stop what they're doing – but once they get to class, they have a great time.

You might even ask yourself if you're doing the right thing by making them go to karate when they don't want to.

When this happens, ask yourself, "Which of these activities is in the best long-term interest of my child?" 'Which will help them create a path to success?" "Which will help develop their character?"

Once you've answered these questions, you'll know that you've made the right decision.

Yours for Successful Kids,

M. Brumitt

Master Brumitt

Letter #20: Positive Role Models

Dear Friends,

Our teachers have a "secret weapon" in developing life skills in our students: Influence. Their influence on the students is so strong that kids who ordinarily have a hard time listening or behaving are surprisingly attentive when in karate class. In fact, parents often ask us why their kids listen more to their karate teachers than they do to their own parents.

So, why do martial arts teachers have so much influence on kids? Sometimes even more than school teachers, and sometimes it even seems like a bigger influence than mom and dad!

It may be because the teachers have what the kids want – a "larger than life" ability to kick, block, punch, and to "take care of business." Some parents even refer to the karate teachers as "real life superheroes" that their children can look up to.

Because of this, kids have a huge desire for recognition from their karate teachers. So when they hear their teachers saying things like cleaning their room, listening to their parents, or getting good grades are important, the kids take it very seriously.

On the other side of this, parents have to contend with the "Law of Familiarity." While kids see our teachers as being almost "super human," they see their parents every day doing those essential, yet mundane things like cleaning, cooking, going to work, and other daily tasks. They almost never see mom or dad doing flying side kick or jump-spinning kicks, or any other cool moves that they see on TV.

Because we recognize the influence that the teachers have on children, I am very selective in whom I choose to work with the students.

In fact, I only hire teachers from our student body – and therefore, each teacher has had a three to four year interview process! I only hire teachers who demonstrate Integrity, Patience, Courtesy, Perseverance, and Compassion, and of course, they have to be a good Martial Artist.

You see, at *"Duane Brumitt's Tri-Star Martial Arts Academy,"* there is so much more to the Martial Arts than just kicking and punching. It is a way to teach successful life skills. And it is important that our teachers "Walk the Walk."

In order for our students to learn these life skills in class, they must be completely present focused. The teacher must keep them focused, physically engaged, and connected emotionally with the teacher.

Naturally, the Martial Arts lend themselves to keeping the children physically engaged. The kids are able to stay mentally focused because we keep our classes fast paced, and involve the kids in drills that are exciting.

Additionally, the teachers don't have to compete with other distractions, like television and friends, so we have the advantage of having the kids' full attention, not to mention the fact that the children desire praise from the teacher.

Now, one thing that sets us apart from other teachers and coaches is that we are always reminding our students not to use their physical Martial Arts skills outside of the karate school. This is different from a piano teacher, who would never tell her students, "Now remember... don't use your piano skills on other kids."

On the other hand, we do encourage the kids to use the mental skills that they learn in karate every day! If you listen, you'll hear the teachers challenge the students at the beginning of class to use the skills described in the Student Creed:

"I intend to develop myself for success - mentally, physically, and spiritually - by avoiding negative habits and attitudes.

I develop self-discipline in order to bring out the best in myself and others.

I use my martial arts constructively and defensively to help myself and my fellow man, and to never be abusive or offensive to myself or others.

Yes…Hollywood has helped our instructors become "larger than life." At the same time, it has increased the impact that our teachers are able to make on children.

Therefore, the stature of our teachers is a great tool for positively impacting children. If you feel that your child would benefit from an outside influence (when it comes to respect, responsibility, or success in other areas of life) just remind them: How would Mr. or Ms. (insert karate instructors name) think about …?"

We are grateful for the duty, honor, and privilege of working with our students at developing the skills necessary to be successful in all areas of their lives!

Yours for Successful Kids,

M. Brumitt

Master Duane Brumitt

Letter #21: Powerful Self-Esteem Building Strategies

Dear Parents,

Here are my all-time favorite 10 Strategies for RAISING the Self-Esteem of your children!

Please take the time to review these ideas with your children!

1. Always, always tell the truth!
2. Take responsibility! If you did something you shouldn't have, admit it! Don't blame others or make excuses!
3. If somebody gives you a compliment, smile and say "Thank you!"
4. Complete assignments early!
5. Avoid negative people; pick friends who have high self-esteem.
6. Help raise the self-esteem of others!
7. Dream big dreams about your future!
8. Be organized, both with time and things, at all times.
9. Be healthy! Exercise regularly. Eat only those foods that are good for you!
10. Pick a couple of activities that are important to you, and MASTER them!

Yours for Successful Kids,

M. Brumitt

Master Duane Brumitt

Letter #22: A Gentle Spirit

Dear Friends,

This is one of my favorite Martial Art stories. I thought you might enjoy it too.

M. Brumitt
Master Duane Brumitt

A Soft Answer

A turning point in my life came one day on a train in the suburbs of Tokyo, in the middle of a drowsy spring afternoon. The old car clanked and rattled over the rails. It was comparatively empty – a few housewives with their kids in tow, some old folks out shopping, a couple of off-duty bartenders studying the racing form. I gazed absently at the drab houses and dusty hedgerows.

At one station the doors opened, and suddenly the quiet afternoon was shattered by a man bellowing at the top of his lungs, yelling violent, obscene, incomprehensible curses. Just as the doors closed, the man, still yelling, staggered into our car. He was big, drunk, and dirty. He wore laborer's clothing. His front was stiff with dried vomit. His eyes bugged out a demonic, neon red. His hair was crusted with filth. Screaming, he swung at the first person he saw, a woman holding a baby. The blow glanced off her shoulder, sending her spinning into the laps of an elderly couple. It was a miracle that the baby was unharmed.

The couple jumped up and scrambled toward the other end of the car. They were terrified. The laborer aimed a kick at the retreating back of the old lady. "I'll kill you, old woman!" he bellowed. He missed, the old woman scuttled to safety. This so enraged the drunk that he grabbed the metal pole in the center of the car and tried to wrench it out of its stanchion. I could see that one of his hands was cut and bleeding. The train lurched ahead, the passengers frozen with fear. I stood up.

I was young and in pretty good shape. I stood six feet, weighed 225. I'd been putting in a solid eight hours of Aikido training every day for the past three years. I liked to throw and grapple. I thought I was tough. Trouble was, my martial skill was untested in actual combat. As students of Aikido, we were not allowed to fight.

My teacher, the founder of Aikido, taught us each morning that martial arts were devoted to peace. "Aikido," he said again and again, "is the art of reconciliation. Whoever has the mind to fight has broken his connection with the universe. If you try to dominate other people, you are already defeated. We study how to resolve conflict, not how to start it."

I listened to his words. I tried hard. I wanted to quit fighting. I even went so far as to cross the street a few times to avoid the chimpira, the pinball punks who lounged around the train stations. They'd have been happy to test my martial ability. My forbearance exalted me. I felt both tough and holy. In my heart of hearts, however, I was dying to be a hero. I wanted a chance, an absolutely legitimate opportunity; whereby I might save the innocent by destroying the guilty.

"This is it!" I said to myself as I got to my feet. "This slob, this animal, is drunk and mean and violent. People are in danger. If I don't do something fast, somebody will probably get hurt. I'm gonna take him to the cleaners."

Seeing me stand up, the drunk saw a chance to focus his rage. "Aha!" he roared: "A foreigner! You need a lesson in Japanese manners!" He punched the metal pole once to give weight to his words.

I held on lightly to the commuter-strap overhead. I gave him a slow look of disgust and dismissal. I gave him every bit of nastiness I could summon up. I planned to take this turkey apart, but he had to be the one to move first. And I wanted him mad, because the madder he got, the more certain the victory. I pursed my lips and blew him a sneering, insolent kiss. It hit him like a slap in the face. "All right!" he hollered. "You're gonna get a lesson." He gathered himself for a rush at me. He'd never know what hit him.

A split-second before he moved, someone shouted "Hey!" It was ear-splitting. I remember being struck by the strangely joyous, lilting quality of it – as though you and a friend had been searching diligently for something, and he had suddenly stumbled upon it. "Hey!"

I wheeled to my left, the drunk spun to his right. We both stared down at a little old Japanese man. He must have been well into his seventies, this tiny gentleman, sitting there immaculate in his kimono and hakama. He took no notice of me but beamed delightedly at the laborer, as though he had a most important, most welcome secret to share.

"C'mere," the old man said in an easy vernacular, beckoning to the drunk, "C'mere and talk with me." He waved his hand lightly. The big man followed, as if on a string. He planted his feet belligerently in front of the old gentleman, and towered threateningly over him. "Talk to you," he roared above the clacking wheels, "Why should I talk to you?" The drunk now had his back to me. If his elbow moved so much as a millimeter, I'd drop him in his socks.

The old man continued to beam at the laborer. There was not a trace of fear or resentment about him. "What'cha been drinkin'?" he asked lightly, his eyes sparkling with interest. "I been drinkin' sake," the laborer bellowed back, "And it's none of your business!" Flecks of spittle spattered the old man.

"Oh, that's wonderful," the old man said with delight, "absolutely wonderful! You see, I love sake, too. Every night, me and my wife (she's 76 you know), we warm up a little bottle of sake and take it out into the garden, and we sit on the old wooden bench that my grandfather's first student made for him. We watch the sun go down, and we look to see how our persimmon tree is doing. My great-grandfather planted that tree, you know, and we worry about whether it will recover from those ice-storms we had last winter. Persimmons do not do well after ice-storms, although I must say that ours has done rather better than I expected, especially when you consider the poor quality of the soil. Still, it is most gratifying to watch when we take our sake and go out to enjoy the evening – even when it rains!" He looked up at the laborer, eyes twinkling, happy to share his delightful information.

As he struggled to follow the intricacies of the old man's conversation, the drunk's face began to soften. His fists slowly unclenched. "Yeah," he said slowly, "I love persimmons, too…" His voice trailed off.

"Yes." Said the old man, smiling, "and I'm sure you have a wonderful wife."

"No," replied the laborer, "My wife died." He hung his head. Very gently, swaying with the motion of the train, the big man began to sob. "I don't got no wife. I don't got no home. I don't got no job. I don't got no money. I don't got nowhere to go. I'm so ashamed for myself." Tears rolled down his cheeks, a spasm of pure despair rippled through his body.

Now it was my turn. Standing there in my well-scrubbed youthful innocence, my make-this-world-safe-for-democracy righteousness, I suddenly felt dirtier than he was.

Just then, the train arrived at my stop. The platform was packed, and the crowd surged into the car as soon as the doors opened. Maneuvering my way out, I heard the old man cluck sympathetically. "My, my," he said with undiminished delight, "that is a very difficult predicament, indeed. Sit down here and tell me about it."

I turned my head for one last look. The laborer was sprawled like a sack on the seat, his head in the old man's lap. The old man looked down at him all compassion and delight, one hand softly stroking the filthy, matted head.

As the train pulled away, I sat down on a bench. What I had wanted to do with muscle and meanness had been accomplished with a few kind words. I had seen Aikido tried in combat, and the essence of it was love, as the founder had said. I would have to practice the art with an entirely different spirit. It would be a long time before I could speak about the resolution of conflict.

By Terry Dobson

Yours for Successful Kids,

Duane Brumitt

Letter #23: Listening Skills

Dear Friends,

It's frustrating when our children don't seem to listen, isn't it?

And when they don't pay attention to what you are saying in the home, you have to wonder how much they are missing at school!

When I began in 1998 to teach Martial Arts in our community, I developed a 5-step approach to develop the skill of listening. You can easily teach these 5-steps to your child!

- The Listening Posture. Teach your child that when it's time to listen, they must sit or stand straight up. Shoulders back. Lift the chest a little. Chin high.
- Direct Eye Contact is Essential. Insist on it. Your child will then be able to focus on the words being said.
- Repeat the message back to the speaker, when possible. For example, a child might say, "So Mom, you'd like me to clean up my room and feed the cat before I play on the computer?" This lets the speaker know your child has understood!
- Ask Questions! Coach your children to ask respectful questions. This shows they are paying attention and care about what the other person is saying!

30 Days to Higher Self-Esteem *For Your Child!*

- Look for more information. Especially with older children, train them to ask themselves, "How does this person feel about what they are saying?" Are they angry? Bored? Interested? Concerned?

My friends, even young children can be taught these steps. Begin by reading these skills to them, and then practicing each skill!

When you observe your child losing focus, just the simple reminder, "Remember…listening skills!" will refocus them.

And, of course, watch like a hawk for situations when your child does listen effectively. Catch them doing it right, and follow up with a huge dose of appreciation like, "Honey, I was so proud of you for listening to what I was saying!"

If you have questions about the 5 Skills of Listening, give me a call; I'd be happy to help! **815-932-5425**

Yours for Successful Kids,

M. Brumitt

Master Duane Brumitt

Letter #24: Self-Esteem Killers

Dear Friends,

I hate to approach anything from a negative point of view. But sometimes it's necessary to speak bluntly - to discuss the negative in order to understand the positive.

The simple fact is…there are things that parents sometimes do that lower their child's self-esteem.

The following are self-esteem killers. If a parent intended (heaven forbid!) or wanted to lower a child's self-esteem, they would:

1. Compare one child with another, especially with siblings.
2. Have super high standards, reward only high levels of progress.
3. Yell – a lot!
4. Assume their child really wants, needs, and deserves all of the freedom they are asking for.

Additionally, they would:

5. Let the child make lots of choices for themselves, especially when they are really young.
6. Neglect to follow through; for example, Mom tells her daughter that a certain rule violation will result in certain consequences. Daughter commits the violation. Mom caves in and doesn't enforce the consequences.

7. Set standards for the kids that Mom & Dad don't hold themselves to.
8. When you catch children aspiring, caution them not to set their sights too high.
9. Be frugal in spending time with your children.

And finally:

10. Assume they will follow your words, rather than your example.

Of course, our job is to turn each of these awful statements into its opposite. Building your child's self-esteem requires consistent effort. Be diligent!

If you have questions about Self-Esteem issues, give me a call; I'd be happy to help! **815-932-5425**

Yours for Successful Kids,

M. Brumitt

Master Duane Brumitt

Letter #25: Popularity Issues

Dear Parents,

A popular person is one who is liked by many people. It's nice to be popular…but the pursuit of popularity can lead to trouble!

Heather says, "I want to be popular no matter what. I'll do whatever it takes!"

Monica says, "I'd like to be popular, of course…but not at any price. I insist on being myself!"

As parents, the thought expressed by "Heather" is bound to make us uneasy. Monica, of course, expresses a healthier perspective.

When popularity becomes too important to your child, problems arise.

- Sometimes children will do things they know they shouldn't do…because they are afraid of losing popularity. They may "cave in" to peer pressure.
- Other times, children will feel that they aren't popular with the "right" crowd. They don't appreciate their current friends.
- Some kids believe that popularity is based on having the "right" clothes, or participating in the "right" activities." They lose their identity by following the crowd.

When these types of popularity are attained, they are shallow and short lasting. They last only until the next "popularity test" comes up.

Teach your child to be a person who does the right thing…no matter what other people think; and the loyalty, integrity, and kindness will lead to genuine popularity!

Teach them to treat all others, regardless of social status, with respect and courtesy. Remind them not to be tricked into doing things they know are wrong in order to gain popularity.

Above all, continually teach about the value and the importance of your relationship to each other within your family. Teach them about your family history and your family heritage.

A young person who has a strong sense of family pride won't succumb to the pressure to be too popular. Popularity will come to your child when people recognize them as a person with integrity!

If you have questions about popularity issues, give me a call; I'd be happy to help! **815-932-5425**

Your Friend,

M. Brumitt

Master Duane Brumitt

Letter #26: Dealing With Fear

Dear Parents,

Fear affects us all, at one time or another. It:

1. Prevents us from doing things we should do, or would like to do.
2. Produces mental stress and physical illness.
3. Robs us of the happy, healthy, confident life we deserve!

But here's a little known secret. Fear is like a toothless dog; all bark and no bite.

Our children must learn that there are two types of fear.

The 1st type is the fear of circumstances that are truly dangerous. This fear is important and must be paid attention to.

Should you have some fear about walking into traffic? Facing a vicious dog? An approaching tornado? You bet!

These fears are there to protect us from situations that might actually harm us!

For most of us, these situations occur infrequently.

The 2nd type of fear is different. It's also much more common.

It's the fear that arises when no danger is actually present. For example, some kids are afraid of:
- meeting new people
- trying new things
- not conforming with other children

These fears must be conquered! They don't protect us from any actual danger. They serve no purpose, other than to hold us back…to keep us from realizing our potential.

Exercise:
1. With your child, identify a situation that would ordinarily cause him to be afraid.

2. Use visualization to "rehearse" the situation…with a successful outcome. Have Matt sit with his eyes closed. You say something like: "Matt, it's your turn to go to the front of the classroom, and talk to the class. You feel so calm. Your muscles are loose. You are breathing easily. You move without hurrying. You actually enjoy your time in front of the class. You finish your presentation, and everybody applauds. You have a huge smile on your face as you return to your seat. You feel so proud of yourself!"

3. Repeat and reinforce this process frequently, each time creating a vivid picture for Matt.

4. Teach Matt to "replay" this mental image on his own.

If you have questions about helping your child conquer FEAR, give me a call at **815-932-5425**. I'd be glad to help!

Your Friend,

Duane Brumitt

Letter #27: Five Skills For Making New Friends!

Dear Parents,

It hurts, doesn't it, when your child has a hard time making friends? Some kids make friends easily; many others need some coaching.

But good news! These important social skills are easy to teach, and easy to rehearse at home.

Practice these strategies with your child:

1. Teach your child to introduce himself to as many people as possible; he might say, for example, "Hi, my name is Trevor…what's yours?" Practice saying this with a SMILE, and a HANDSHAKE!

2. Remind your child to ask questions when they've met somebody new, to find out what type of things their new friend is interested in. Help your child understand how to encourage their new friend to talk about their interests!

    Rehearse questions like:
    "So, what kind of stuff do you like to do?"
    And
    "What did you do last weekend?"

3. It's OK to make friends with kids who are popular, but remind your child to also look for new friends among the kids who are less popular. Watch for kids who are eating, walking, or playing alone!

4. Sometimes kids try to rush things too much in the early stages of friendship. Point out that good friendships are often developed slowly!

5. Explain to your child that EVERYBODY, at times, is shy about making new friends…encourage your child to take the initiative. Remind him that his BEST FRIENDS were once his NEW FRIENDS!

6. And, of course, the best way to HAVE a friend is to BE a friend! Remind your child to be polite, interested, helpful, and fun to be around!

Rehearse these strategies a couple of times each week, and your child will learn to make friends easily!

Sincerely,

Duane Brumitt

Letter #28: No Substitute For Time

Dear Fellow Parents,

Once again, a series of tragic events in the world grabs the attention of parents everywhere.

Questions, such as, "What do we do to prevent this from happening again?" and "How do we protect our children?" are on everybody's minds.

Community leaders will be debating whether or not anything can be done.

I don't know what the answer is to this national problem. However, on a very local level – within each of our homes, there is a lot we can do.

Move closer to your kids. If you are already close, move even closer. Developing and maintaining the rapport, communication, and honesty that prevents these tragedies takes a lot of work.

There is an age when children, particularly teens, try to pull away – and become a little harder to hold close than it was when they were young children. However, this is when your children need you the most!

There comes an age when it's not "cool" to have Mom and Dad around. "Give us our independence!" the kids cry. They become very persuasive…but don't give in.

It is a scary world out there for kids. And I believe that most kids, deep down, know that they really do need the close relationship they had with their parents. They need advice, correction, rules, and guidance to negotiate the very uncertain waters of their teen years.

Kids, all the way through high school, and well into young adulthood, can benefit from close relationships with parents.

So what is the key? Simple… Time. At exactly the same moment that both you and your kids are swamped with other activities; at the same moment when they tend to pull away…that's when they need your time the most!

There is no substitute for time spent with you! In a short time, your kids will be out of the house, and on their own. I encourage you to make the best use of the remaining years. Your children may resist. After all, they have to appear to be "cool." But don't give in. Pull them close, they will thank you for it. Someday!

Your friend,

Duane Brumitt

Letter #29: Powerful Confidence

Dear Parents,

> *"Karate helps develop our students' confidence."*

That's a pretty big claim, isn't it? Many parents have asked us what exactly we do to develop confidence in their children.

A lot of people think that students develop confidence because they are learning self-defense skills. But that's only a small part of it.

If you've been watching, you may have noticed that one of the first things we teach our students is how to have a good sense of balance. Balance is at the root of developing confidence. It's also one of the main reasons why kids are sometimes more reserved, and hold back. After all…who wants to stumble in front of their peers?

The only time anyone really pays attention to balance in children is in that awkward, learning how to ride a bike stage. Few activities in a child's life will actively teach the skills of balance.

In my experience with my own children, I've found that every one of my children's coaches, without exception, assumed that the kids on his team already had balance and coordination – and focused only on the skills necessary to make the team win (hitting the ball, passing, strategy, etc.)

In Martial Arts, however, balance is an important part of what we do, particularly when learning how to kick. Just watch any beginners in class, and you'll see how important balance is. Many beginning students "touch down" when they're kicking…placing a foot on the ground to regain balance before executing their kick. Balance is like a muscle – the more you work it, the stronger it becomes.

Coordination goes hand in hand with balance. Like with balance, a lack of coordination can result in self-doubt. If a child is always awkward, stumbling, and knocking things down, they will know it, and begin to feel self-doubt. This is why we spend so much time working on both fine and gross motor skills. In fact, we strive for our students; by the time they reach Black Belt, to be equally as coordinated with their right hand as their left foot!

While all these things are very important, there is also much more to developing confidence than basic physical skills.

There are psychological skills…

One way we teach our students the "ABC's of Conflict Avoidance" is by doing various role-playing with the kids. It's exciting to watch their eyes light up when they learn ways to outsmart, trick, or talk their way out of a dangerous situation.

Our students learn that the best way to win a fight is to use their heads. They are taught to either 1) Recognize and avoid dangerous situations, or 2) Negotiate, talk, or trick a way out of the situation.

As the students learn more advanced routines, their confidence grows. They begin to feel like "I can do this," "I can block a punch," or "Wow, I'm getting better all the time!" We teach the karate moves in small amounts…and when the students grow confident with them, we teach them more. During the week before their belt promotion, we review all of the things they have learned so that they will be confident and look their best at their promotion.

In fact, their belt promotion is one of our "secret weapons" in developing confidence. Speaking or performing in public is one of the biggest fears that many people have. And in order for a student to receive a belt promotion, they must pass their "belt test" by performing in front of their teachers, families, and friends. They have to face their fear…and conquer it!

BUT…we set the kids up for success. *"Duane Brumitt's Tri-Star Martial Arts Academy"* doesn't believe in failing anyone publicly in the beginning…so during each month's "Stripe Week," we quiz the students and make sure that their skills are up to par.

If a student needs help, we provide free private lessons to help them. So by the time they get to their belt promotion, it's an automatic win. All the student needs to do is show up at the ceremony and do their moves.

Few things can boost self-confidence like facing a fear and coming out successful. That's why our belt promotions are so important to developing confidence.

And, of course, being able to "take care of business" – by knowing physical Martial Arts skills – helps confidence as well.

Yours for Successful Kids,

M. Brumitt

Master Duane Brumitt

Letter #30: Smell The Roses

Dear Parents,

Hello, my friends…hope you are well! Boy life gets busier and busier doesn't it? Especially when so many events are packed together sometimes.

Here at *"Duane Brumitt's Tri-Star Martial Arts Academy,"* for example, we always have something happening each month. Busy, busy busy!!!

We are not complaining…on the contrary! We like being busy!

However, as I prepare a "Message of the Week" (The Importance of Being Happy), I am reminded of the importance, and sometimes the difficulty of, maintaining a happy, positive outlook.

Looking forward is good – wouldn't you agree? In fact, if we are not good at looking ahead, we are headed for trouble. But sometimes we become TOO future focused…and forget to look around at all the splendid things that are taking place around us.

So…take a few minutes…take a deep breath…take a good look at the people around you…and think for a minute about the abundant life we have been given.

Express some appreciation to the people who are important to you…and, while you are at it, remember to give some thanks to the Source of all good things… Jesus Christ!

Your Friend,

M. Brumitt

Master Brumitt

Letter #31: Pursuit Of Excellence

Dear Students,

I would like to speak to you about Black Belt Excellence. You understand how it works, right? You begin by setting high standards for yourself in the Martial Arts. You work hard, overcome obstacles, and reach your goals. And, in the process, you begin to see that you can apply these same standards of excellence in the other areas of your life…home, school, career, etc.

You have achieved Black Belt Excellence when you hold high standards for yourself in ALL areas! Committing to excellence in one area will impact other areas.

But here is a warning: It works the other way, too. Settling for mediocrity in ANY area of your life will impact all other areas! Let's say you are motivated to excel in Martial Arts. You have committed to excellence. But you have another area of your life that might not be so important to you, right now. Maybe academics or personal relationships. And you let yourself be content with mediocrity in this area. You allow neglect to slip in. You are in danger!

Mediocrity and neglect, once they are allowed to enter your life, will quickly move to those areas that ARE important to you…even if you have already committed to excellence!

The lesson is this: Tolerate NO mediocrity; tolerate NO neglect. Dedicate yourself to Black Belt Excellence in every area of your life!

Remember that a Black Belt is just a White Belt that never Quit!

Your Friend,

M. Brumitt

Master Brumitt

Letter #32: A Thoughtful Review

Dear Students,

Yipes! What a fast year! It seems like just last month that it was New Year's Day morning, and then a bunch of stuff happened…and now it's December!

The holidays are always a nice time to step back, take a deep breath…and relax. It's a terrific time for reviewing the past year.

Was it the year I hoped for? Did I stay focused on the things that were important to me? Did I contribute?

Did I grow? Did I take care of those entrusted to me? Did I make it my business to care for and encourage those around me?

What do I expect of myself in the coming year? How will I conduct myself? How will I be toward the people that are most important to my life? How will I handle stress and adversity?

If I could "design" myself any way that I want…how would I be?

My friends, take some time this holiday season to tackle these powerful questions. Some of my most important and defining moments have been when I was sitting quietly, with a pad of paper and a pen – reflecting, making notes, and designing the life that I hoped to live.

May the joy and peace of this special season be yours…

    God's Blessings to You My Friend,

M. Brumitt
    Master Brumitt

BONUS: 104 Ways To Positively Reinforce Your Child!

There is a language of encouragement... a language that can be used to raise a child's self-esteem! And – unfortunately – many people lack words in this important language!

Use these phrases, as often as possible, to build your child's confidence!

Two important reminders:
a. Remember to praise approximations of success. Don't wait until your child "hits the bull's-eyes" before providing encouragement!
b. When possible, praise your child publicly!

1. Excellent work!
2. I'm so proud of you!
3. You always give it your best effort!
4. I admire your determination!
5. You never quit, do you?
6. I can't wait to tell Mom about your progress!
7. You were really hustling out there!
8. I think this was your best time so far!
9. I'm inspired by your commitment!
10. You have such high standards for yourself!
11. Well done!
12. Keep up the good work!
13. Marvelous effort!
14. You nailed it!
15. Just like a pro!
16. What is the secret of your success?
17. You were a tiger out there today!

18. You really set a fine example!
19. Excellent leadership!
20. We are so proud of you!
21. You were really focused!
22. You are becoming more responsible every day!
23. I'm your biggest fan!
24. High Five!
25. Tell us how you did that!
26. Will you show us again?
27. How did you feel at the moment of victory?
28. We are really behind you!
29. I admire the way you handled this setback!
30. You really hit the bull's-eye there!
31. You are in the groove now!
32. Stay with it – you are doing just fine!
33. Dig down deep ... I know you can make it!
34. You really showed us something out there!
35. You really "wowed" them out there!
36. You had them in the palm of your hand!
37. You looked so poised – so confident!
38. Where did you learn to do that so well?
39. You are on a roll now!
40. You have an excellent memory!
41. You act so grown up around the younger children!
42. I have a lot of confidence in you!
43. You have my trust!
44. Now that's a job well done!
45. You have become so organized!
46. My hat is off to you!
47. You deserve a big round of applause!
48. Now that is excellent work!
49. Your politeness really sets a good example!
50. You always set a good example!
51. That is really focused effort!

52. We are proud to have you in our family!
53. I knew you could do it!
54. You set some pretty high standards for yourself!
55. Awesome!
56. Tremendous effort!
57. You da man/woman!
58. Incredible!
59. Superb job!
60. You've got it now!
61. That's using the old brain pal!
62. A+!
63. Marvelous work!
64. You pay such attention to detail!
65. You hold yourself to a high standard, don't you?
66. Magnificent!
67. You are on fire!
68. You slam-dunked that one!
69. Show me again how you did that!
70. Bravo!
71. Take a bow!
72. Let's go show Dad how you did that!
73. Why don't you call grandma & tell her about your victory?
74. Muy Bueno!
75. That was super-mega-fantastic-turbo-awesome!
76. You were so poised!
77. You are always brave when trying new things!
78. You're the man!
79. You do such careful work!
80. That was much better than before!
81. Now you're getting it!
82. You were unstoppable!
83. You really showed us something out there!
84. This is first-rate work!

30 Days to Higher Self-Esteem *For Your Child!*

85. You really took it to them!
86. You handled that with a lot of maturity!
87. You are a class act!
88. You make it look so easy!
89. I know how hard you tried!
90. You've pushed through every obstacle!
91. You are really making progress!
92. I admire your tenacity!
93. You have such a commitment to excellence!
94. Excellent brain-work!
95. You are a quick learner!
96. Your memory is excellent!
97. You are quick on your feet!
98. I admire your generosity!
99. You've really improved!
100. You aced it!
101. You are a blessing!
102. You are an excellent example to your brother & sister!
103. God has given you a real gift in… (fill in the blank)!
104. You are designed for accomplishment, engineered for success and endowed with the seeds of greatness! (Zig Ziglar's Quote)

My advice would be to pick one of the 104 ways per week, use it with your child or children for that week. Do this for every week for the next 104 weeks (two years) and you will see amazing things with them when you start positively reinforcing them.

THANK YOU

Thank you for reading this book. I hope you found more than what you were looking for out of it. If you have any questions or would like help please contact me. I would be happy to help.

(815) 932-5425

Free Offers and Resources From Duane Brumitt

FREE Booklet
BRAND NEW: Positive Parenting
STRATAGIES

Simple Strategies To Help Your Kids Thrive!

Get ALL 4 FREE - eBook, Workbook, Executive Summary, CD!

www.TriStarKarate.com/PPS

32 Letters From Karate Master Duane Brumitt to His Students & Their Parents!

FREE Booklet

Do You Dream Of Forever Fixing Your Child's Weight Problem? Heart Break? Enough Is Enough! Are You Hanging On "The Thin Line?"

Well Then, NOW Is The Time To Get Down To Some Details On How You Can Get Control Back In Your Lives... And Adopt Sane Ways To Help Your Child... And Start Making Sense Out Of The Chaos!

Get The Step-By-Step Plan FREE @
www.TriStarKarate.com/HealthyKids

FREE Booklet

Child Safety Online:

Top Tips to Protect Your Child from Online Predators!

Is Your Child At Risk Of Being Lured By A Stranger Online?

Discover How You Can Prevent Your Child From Becoming A Predator's Target And Your Worst Nightmare Coming True! Get Yours FREE!

www.TriStarKarate.com/SafeKids

ATTENTION:

FREE KARATE

Nearly Everyone Has Thought
About Karate For Themselves Or Their Children.
Now You Can Discover
If Karate Is Right For You...At No Risk Or Expense!

FREE 30 DAY MEMBERSHIP

We Want You To Be Sure Karate Is Everything
You Want Or Need!
So We'll Train You Or Your Child For 30 Days For Free!

FREE Gift #1:
"Exclusive" 30 Days of Martial Arts Training at Duane Brumitt's Tri-Star Martial Arts Academy
(Value $169.00)
During this time frame you will be able to experience what our martial arts program has to offer.

> 30 Days of
> **Martial Arts Training**
> At
> **Duane Brumitt's**
> Tri-Star Martial Arts Academy
> **For FREE**

FREE Gift #2:
An "Official" Tri-Star Martial Arts Karate Uniform
(Value $40.00)
This uniform is yours to keep even if you decide that our program is not right for you.

FREE Gift #3:
The DVD entitled "In Their Own Words"
(Value $19.95)
This DVD will take you through the back door of our school allowing you to see and hear firsthand from parents and students just like you.

FREE Gift #4:
The Self-Protection Call entitled "Safety in the Home"
(Value $77.00)
In this call we will cover how to burglar-proof your home, burglar proof your behavior, and protect your personal information.

FREE Gift #5:
The Self-Protection Call entitled "Safety Outside the Home"
(Value $77.00)
We will cover how to train to protect yourself and your family, how to train your senses, learn effective distraction techniques, and discover your safety zones.

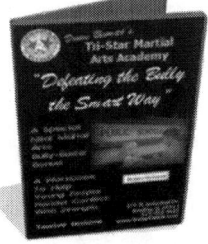

FREE Gift #6:
The "Bully-Buster" Tele-Seminar Call
(Value $47.00)
During this call you will discover for your child the mental art of self-defense, the three lines of self-defense, the 12 bully buster basic tools and how your child can be a victor and not a victim.

Total Value: $429.95

Take a Video Tour, Get all the Details, and Claim your FREE Gifts at:

www.FreeKarate.info

Goal Realization Made Easy: Your Guidebook to Lasting Happiness

Happiness will help you focus on clear goals and will teach you how to actualize them by using the proper mindset and behavior.

It will steadily steer you in the right direction so that you can attain the results you really want.

It is true that all successful people and millionaires/billionaires have goals, and they know how to reach them. Wouldn't it be great if you can actually acquire their attitudes and be on the right track to success too?

You certainly can!

Oder your copy of Goal Realization Made Easy right now and be a goal achiever for life. It's easier than you think... once you know the right steps to take.

www.GoalSettingMadeEasy.com

Resources

- Professor Paul Pilzer, *"Other People's Money"* (Simon & Schuster; First Printing, Underlining edition October 1989), 5

- Ann Landers column, 7/21/86, 15

- W. Livingston Larned, *"Father Forgets"*, (Published 1927), 42

- Terry Dobson, *"A Soft Answer"* from Safe and Alive, (Published 1982), 57

Made in the USA
Charleston, SC
04 September 2016